Word Play Sm

by David Orme

Contents

Section 1
Sounds I like – consonant sounds	2
Tongue Twisters for People with Twisty Tongues – tongue twisters	4
One-letter Poems – visual/verbal puns	5
Riddles – imagery	6
The F Zoo – consonant sounds	7
New Nursery Rhymes – rhymes	8
High Job, Low Job – opposites	9

Section 2
Getting to the Other Side – riddle	10
Silly Bubble Creatures – syllable counting	11
Being Things – personification	12
Keep on Scratching – rhymes: phoneme *e*	14
Magic Letter – final *e*	15
Pool People – alliteration	16

Section 3
Shh! Silent Letters – silent letters: *g* and *k*	17
Don't Make Me Laugh – jokes: puns, word play	18
Soap in Your Soup – parody	20
Missing Letters – vocabulary puzzle	22
Chomp! – digraph *ch*	23
Glossary of Words from the Contents Page	24

Longman

Edinburgh Gate
Harlow, Essex

Sounds I Like

MMM!

Say me when you eat chocolate:

MMMMMMMMMMMMM!

Or soak in a hot bath:

MMMMMMMMMMMM!

Or kick off your shoes
After a hard day:

MMMMMMMMMMMM!

Say me again,
You know you like me:

MMMMMMMMMMM!

Such a Stupid Snake

I'm such a stupid snake

I wish I could speak better

I try so hard it makes me cross

But I can only say one letter!

Tongue Twisters for People with Twisty Tongues

Laura Loves Lollies

Laura Loot loves yellow lollies
Really licks them lots,
But Lily Lewis is allergic –
Look at all her spots!

Shining Shoes

Sam shines Sue's shoes,
Sue shines Sam's shoes
Sam sings 'Shining shoes'
Sue sings too.

One-letter Poems

Riddles

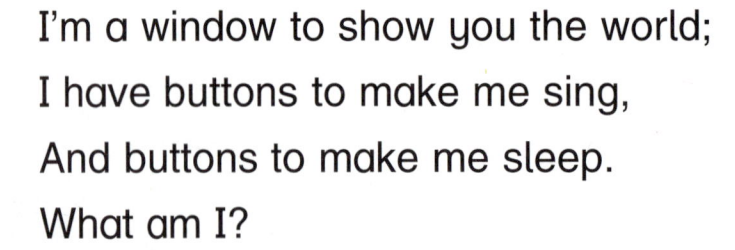

I'm a window to show you the world;
I have buttons to make me sing,
And buttons to make me sleep.
What am I?

I'm an elephant's head:
I squirt water on flowers
Through my long trunk.
What am I?

You can't see me
You can't touch me
You can't see me,
But when I'm in the mood
I'm strong enough
To knock you flat!
Who am I?

I can make you take your coat off
Without touching you!
Who am I?

Answers: television set, watering can, wind, sun

The F Zoo

We've got
Fat ones
Friendly ones
Fierce ones
and
Fluffy ones!

Fast ones
Feathered ones
Fishy ones
and
Fancy ones!

Flat ones
Funny ones
Frightening ones
Floppy ones!

And these are just a few
Of the fantastic creatures
You can find
At the Fabulous
F zoo!

New Nursery Rhymes

Humpty Dumpty sat on the wall
Humpty Dumpty had a great fall
All the king's horses and all the king's men
Had scrambled egg for breakfast again.

Little Miss Muffet
Sat on a tuffet
Eating a plate of stew;
Along came a spider
Who sat down beside her –
She ate up the spider, too.

High Job, Low Job

Mr Long has a high job:

He's the man in the cab on the tallest crane,

Every morning he climbs to the top,

And every night he comes down again.

Mr Short has a low job:

He's the man who inspects the sewers and drains;

Every morning he climbs to the bottom,

And every night he comes up again!

Getting to the Other Side

My first's in cat, but not in kite,
My second's in hat, and twice in height,
My third sounds like what's either side of your nose,
My fourth's in comes, but not in goes.
My fifth starts the thing that opens a door,
My sixth's at the end when you ask for more,
My last is in newt but never in toad,

Now why did this creature cross the road?

Silly Bubble Creatures

No one likes me, why is that?
I'm like a big mouse,
    I must be a (...)

Hopping through grass is my regular habit,
I live in a burrow,
    I'm called a (...)

I'm from Australia, How do you do?
I've a baby in my pouch,
    I'm a (...)

A horn on my nose, as strong as a bus,
Watch out, for I'm a (...)

"We're extinct, which is very sad for us,
Now we're nothing but bones!"
    Said the (Tyran...)

Being Things

If I Were the Moon

If I were the moon

I would come out during the day

To annoy the sun,

I would peep through everyone's
   window

To see what television programme
   they were watching,

And I would paint the sky with copies
   of myself

So the night would be full of moons,

And no one would know which one

Was me!

What a Mess

"Just look at me,"
said the world to the sun.
I'm a real mess!
I haven't had a good tidy up
For ages!
I'm really ashamed;
My continents are wearing thin,
And my seas are so disgusting
All the fish are complaining.
As for my forests,
I just don't know what's happened to them.
One day, I really must do something
About it, or
You won't see me
For dust.

Keep on Scratching

Fleas

Displease

When they crawl with such ease

Up her legs to her knees!

How she'll freeze

When she sees

That horrid species

Jumping like chimpanzees

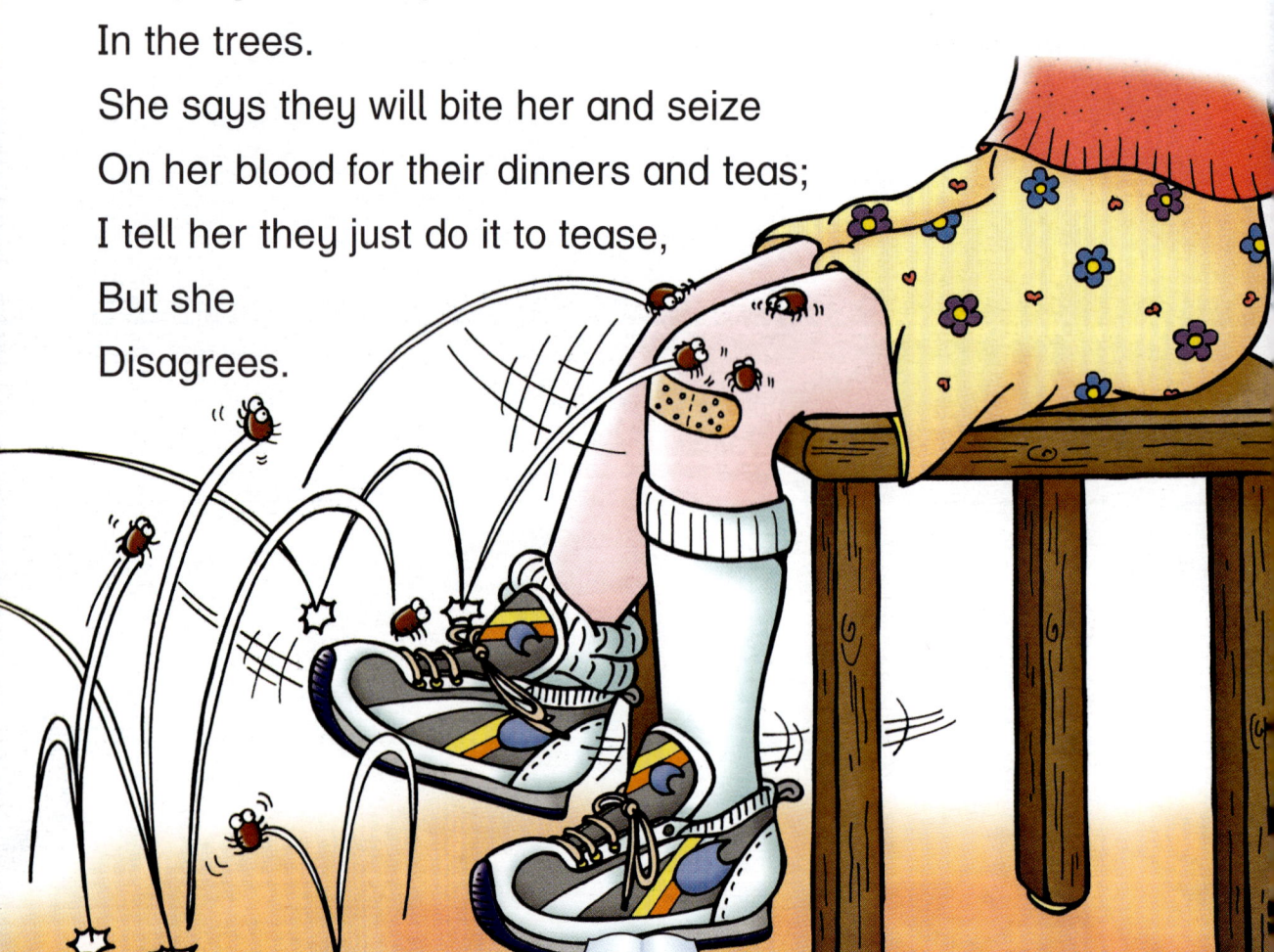

In the trees.

She says they will bite her and seize

On her blood for their dinners and teas;

I tell her they just do it to tease,

But she

Disagrees.

Magic Letter

Do you …
    Hate hats?
    Really rate rats?
    Rip open bananas when they're yellow and ripe,
    Blow your orange pips down a pipe?

Do you …
    Make kites out of kits,
    And bite your Mum though
    You love her to bits?
    You can't do any of these things

Without me
Who am I?
The letter …

Pool People

Debbie dives down at the deep end,
Freddie loves playing the fool,
Tim tickles toes when he sees them,
Which annoys everyone in the pool.

Sue has a smart yellow swimsuit,
Mike has a snorkel and mask,
Lee is an expert life-saver,
If you need to be rescued just ask!

Barry is brilliant at backstroke,
Christine is cool at the crawl,
Donald's a demon at diving,
But Samantha can't swim at all!

Shh! Silent Letters

Gnora is a gnawing gnome
Gnoisily gnibbling all day.

Gnatasha is a gnasty gnome,
We gnow she gnever wants to play.

Gnigel is a football gnome
gneatest of the kickers,

Gnatalie is a gnaughty gnome
Shows her gnice gnew gnickers!

Knock knock!
"Who's there?"

"Knights knitting knots.
Knights with knobbly knees knitting knots.
Knights whose knobbly knots need unknitting.
Knights who don't know how to unknit their knots!"

"Knives unknit knots."

"Have you got a knife?"
"No!"

Don't Make Me Laugh

"I'm an adder," said the snake.

"I'm a multiplier," said the photocopier.

"I'm a divider," said the wall.

"I'm a take-away," said the pizza.

Why is cold slower than hot?
> Because you can catch cold!

Why do children go to school?
> Because the school can't come to them!

Why can't a pony speak?
> Because it's a little hoarse!

Why do firemen wear red braces?
> To make sure their trousers don't fall down!

What do frogs like to drink?
> Croaka Cola!

What would a famous pig give you?
> A snortograph!

What is the difference between a storm and a lion with toothache?
> One pours with rain and the other roars with pain.

What is the difference between an elephant and a letterbox?
> Well, if you don't know I won't send you to post a letter!

Soap in Your Soup

Beautiful soup

Beautiful soup, so rich and green,
Waiting in a hot tureen!
Who for such dainties would not stoop?
Soup of the evening, beautiful Soup!
Soup of the evening, beautiful Soup!
Beau---ootiful Soup!
Beau---ootiful Soup!
Soo---oop of the e---e---evening,
Beautiful, beautiful Soup!

Beautiful Soup! Who cares for fish,
Game, or any other dish?
Who would not give all else for two
pennyworth only of beautiful Soup?
Pennyworth only of beautiful Soup?
beau---ootiful Soup!
beau---ootiful Soup!
Soo---oop of the e---e---evening,
Beautiful, beauti---FUL SOUP!

From *Alice's Adventures in Wonderland* by Lewis Carroll

Beautiful Soap

Beautiful soap, so pure and white,
Who's going to have a bath tonight?
Who's going to soak in a hot frothy tub?
Who's going to give my back a scrub?
Soap of the evening, beautiful soap!
Soap of the evening, beautiful soap!
Beau - ootiful soap! Beau - ootiful soap!
Soap of the evening,
Beautiful, beautiful soap!

Beautiful soap, was it son,
Was it daughter,
Who let it go soggy,
Left in the water?
It's all gone to waste! let us mourn, let us mope
For the squishy white blob
That once was the soap!
Beau - ootiful soap! Beau - ootiful soap!
Soap of the evening,
Beautiful, Beauti - FUL SOAP!

Missing Letters

A poem about food written by a man who had lost the key on his computer that comes between K and M so he had to use a T instead.

Tucy and Bitty tove tiquorice,
Tenny and Testie do not,
Taura and Timmy tike tangerines,
Do Tarry and Ten?
Not a tot.
Tinda and Terry tick totties,
Temon and time,
On a stick,
Tommy and Jutie think jetty
Is tikety to make you feet sick.
Taurence and Teddy tike custard that's tumpy,
With tovety skin on the top,
Tony and Testor tike jettied eets
But Tionet says it's
Just stop.

Chomp!

I like chicken.

I like chicken and chips.

I like chicken and chips and cheese.

I like chicken and chips and cheese and chewing gum.

I like chicken and chips and cheese and chewing gum and cherries and chocolate.

I like chicken and chips and cheese and chewing gum and cherries and chocolate and Chinese crispy noodles.

I like chicken and chips and cheese and chewing gum and cherries and chocolate and Chinese crispy noodles and chestnuts.

I like chicken and chips and cheese and chewing gum and cherries and chocolate and Chinese crispy noodles and chestnuts – in chilli sauce!

I like chicken and chips and cheese and chewing gum and cherries and chocolate and Chinese crispy noodles and chestnuts in chilli sauce –

And don't forget the chutney!

Glossary of Words from the Contents Page

consonant	any letter except *a e i o* and *u*
imagery	a writer's use of words to produce effects
rhymes	words which sound the same, e.g. white/might or ball/fall
tongue twister	something that is difficult to say quickly and correctly
verbal	to do with spoken words
visual	to do with sight and seeing

alliteration	repeating the same phoneme or letter sound in groups of words
final e	when the e at the end of a word changes the vowel sound, e.g. mat – mate; bit – bite
personification	to represent an idea or a thing as a person
phoneme	the smallest unit of sound in a word
riddle	a question, statement or poem which is a puzzle for the reader to solve
syllable	a word or part of a word which has one vowel sound when you say it, e.g. cat (one syllable), rabbit (two)

digraph	two letters representing one sound, e.g. *ch*oose or b*oi*l
joke	something said or done to make people laugh
parody	an imitation which makes fun of something
pun	a play on words, e.g. same sound but different meanings
silent letters	letters in words which have no sound, e.g. knit, reign
vocabulary puzzle	a puzzle which depends on knowing the right words